I0799521

BIG WAVE
SURFING

The Eddie Aikau Big Wave Invitational surf contest in Waimea Bay, Hawaii, in February 2016

# BIG WAVE SURFING

ODYSSEYS

JORDAN FARGO

CREATIVE EDUCATION · CREATIVE PAPERBACKS

Published by Creative Education and Creative Paperbacks
P.O. Box 227, Mankato, Minnesota 56002
Creative Education and Creative Paperbacks are imprints of The Creative Company.
www.thecreativecompany.us

Design and art direction by Graham Morgan
Edited by Kremena Spengler

Images by Alamy Stock Photo/Cinematic Collection, 64, David Olsen, cover; Getty Images/Allen J. Schaben, 39, American Stock Archive, 19, Donald Miralle, 34–35, Nisa Maier, 24, Octavio Passos, 12, Richard Hallman, 52, Ryan Pierse, 56, SOPA Images, 20, 70–71, TIM MCKENNA, 59, Tony Heff, 48, 72, VW Pics, 27; Pexels/Master Cowley, 75, Pixabay, 11; Public Domain/63; Unsplash/ Lucas Davies, 8, tatonomusic, 30; Wikimedia Commons/A. R. Gurrey, Jr., 29, Anthony Quintano, 2, Axel Malmström, 47, John Van Hamersveld, 66, John Robert McPherson, 51, Lookitt, 6, Public Domain, 14, Shalom Jacobovitz/ Brocken Inaglory, 60, Stephanie Martin, 4–5, troy_williams, 69

Copyright © 2025 Creative Education, Creative Paperbacks
International copyright reserved in all countries. No part of this book may be reproduced in any form without written permission from the publisher.

Library of Congress Cataloging-in-Publication Data
Names: Fargo, Jordan, author.
Title: Big wave surfing / Jordan Fargo.
Description: Mankato, Minnesota : Creative Education and Creative Paperbacks, [2025] | Series: Odysseys in extreme sports | ATOS 7 | Includes bibliographical references and index. | Audience: Ages 12-15 years | Audience: Grades 7-9 | Summary: "Ride the towering waves with this title for high school readers about big wave surfing, the thrilling sport of conquering massive swells. Includes skills and equipment needed, a glossary, index, and further resources"– Provided by publisher.
Identifiers: LCCN 2024025234 (print) | LCCN 2024025235 (ebook) | ISBN 9798889893110 (lib. bdg.) | ISBN 9781682776773 (paperback) | ISBN 9798889894223 (ebook)
Subjects: LCSH: Surfing–Juvenile literature. | Waves–Juvenile literature. | Olympics–Juvenile literature.
Classification: LCC GV840.S8 F27 2025 (print) | LCC GV840.S8 (ebook) | DDC 797.3/2-dc23/eng/20240711
LC record available at https://lccn.loc.gov/2024025234
LC ebook record available at https://lccn.loc.gov/2024025235

Printed in China

Surfers enjoy waves along the coastline of Cape Town, South Africa.

Teahupo'o, Tahiti

## CONTENTS

# Introduction

Soured on soccer? Fed up with football? Bored by baseball? Turned off by team sports? If so, extreme sports might be more to your liking. While there is no exact definition of what makes a sport "extreme," the following characteristics, or at least most of them, seem to be common: a higher degree of risk despite use of protective gear; emphasis on achieving high speeds and/or heights; more likely to be performed alone or with a handful of friends; no issues with playing time as in team sports; stunts requiring substantial amounts of skill and practice; less emphasis on formal rules; and an **adrenaline** rush from physical exertion.

**OPPOSITE:** A surfer leaves the ocean at sunset at Ocean Beach, San Diego, California.

One of the most popular extreme sports in the United States, particularly on the West Coast, is surfing. Big wave surfing is an offshoot of regular surfing, where surfers paddle (or are towed) into the **troughs** of waves at least 20 feet (6 meters) tall. Their surfboards are commonly referred to as "guns" or "rowboats." It has become a respected sport because of the extreme heights that waves can reach and the bravery of surfers who ride them.

Love the ocean and the thrill of **shredding** a monster wave along the beach? Then surfing may be just for you. If catching smaller waves by the beach doesn't give you the rush

Surfing big waves requires complete commitment.

ACF77889

**OPPOSITE** Jet skis can help surfers match the speed of massive waves.

you're looking for, then you may be a big wave surfer. It takes a lot of training to master the surfing technique and plenty of patience to wait for the perfect wave.

Big wave surfing requires guts, and the ability to hold your breath for a long period of time. **Paddling out** in big surf can humble even the most gifted athletes, but it's all worth it for that perfect wave. Once you've got it, you must commit to it and surf fast—every second counts. Wait too long and you may end up **wiping out**—or worse.

DUKE

## A Swell in the Making

When you think of the words "founding father," you probably think of people like George Washington or Thomas Jefferson—not a Hawaiian man who spent most of his days out on the ocean. There are quite a few individuals who led to the rise of big wave surfing as we know it today, but many people consider the founding father of modern surfing to be Duke Kahanamoku from Oahu, Hawaii.

**OPPOSITE:** Duke Kahanamoku

He was both a surfing expert and a swimming champion, and his love for the water earned him the title of "Ambassador of Aloha." One of Kahanamoku's biggest accomplishments was his introduction of modern **shortboard** surfing to Australia in 1914. The sport quickly gained popularity and began to reach other places throughout the world. The massive rise in surfing's popularity earned Kahanamoku a spot in both the Swimming and Surfing Hall of Fame.

Though Kahanamoku was a key player in surfing's growth in the 1900s, the activity had already been a beloved pastime in Hawaii for hundreds of years. There is even evidence that surfing and surfboards were present in ancient Polynesian culture thousands of years ago! Hawaiians of all social classes would come together and catch some waves on the southern shores of Oahu, near what is today Honolulu. Waikiki Beach was the most famous of these beaches, and it became a popular destination for many of the world's best surfers. Even though societal norms had separated people into different categories, Hawaiians were all still united through their love for the water.

Historian John R.K. Clark states in his book, *Hawaiian Surfing: Traditions from the Past,* that, "During the 1800s, Hawaiian and non-Hawaiian writers described surfing as a 'national pastime,' a phrase that highlights the prominence surfing held among native Hawaiians." He later goes on to say that "surfing was an activity everyone enjoyed—men, women, and children, chiefs and commoners. The phrase 'national pastime' suggests that surfing was not only widely practiced, but that it was one of the most beloved activities of the Hawaiian people."

In the 1940s and 1950s, surfing was rapidly becoming well known to the rest of the world. The rise of television and sports broadcasts following World War II (1939–1945) helped start and popularize large surfing competitions in Oahu. Surfers from Australia, the U.S., and other countries would gather there to try their hand at catching the world's largest waves. Surfboards were quickly improving, thanks to advances in technology. The world's best surfers wanted to catch even larger, more powerful **swells**. This is where a few more important names entered the mix.

George Downing, Wally Froiseth, Woody Brown, and Buzzy Trent are widely known as pioneers of big wave surfing. They were some of the first surfers to try surfing the monster waves at Makaha, Oahu. Makaha's waves frequently reached heights of 20–30 feet (6–9 m), which were thought to be impossible to ride at the

Surfers in 1960

## An Absolute MONSTER

The largest recorded wave in history reached a devastating height of 1,720 feet (524 m). That's taller than both the Empire State Building and the Eiffel Tower! This mega **tsunami** occurred in Lituya Bay, Alaska, back in 1958, and was triggered by a magnitude 7.8 earthquake. Though the starting wave's **crest** was only 100–300 feet (30–90 m) tall, the subsequent breaking wave along the coast ended up reaching 1,720 feet (524 m). Two people aboard a small fishing boat lost their lives, but, somehow, two other fishing crews lived. Call that a lucky break!

time. Prior to these men hitting the water, surfboards just were not built to maneuver along larger waves. In 1950, Downing developed the first big wave "elephant gun" surfboard, according to sports author John Long. This board was more streamlined than other boards at the time and could handle larger 30-foot (9-meter) waves. Downing also invented the bailout technique, which involves jumping off a surfboard before being hit by a big wave, thus avoiding a nasty **wipe out**. The technique made bigger waves more accessible and eventually helped break a barrier in the world of surfing.

In the 1960s and 1970s, as technology developed and new surfboards enabled surfers to ride larger waves, the recognition and appreciation for the sport grew as well. Surfers from California, in particular, who grew up near the water, began to practice surfing at a young age.

Their love for the water would sometimes draw them to Hawaii, where they could enhance their surfing skills and push themselves to the limit. Teahupo'o in Tahiti, French Polynesia, an overseas territory of France, is another beloved spot. It has waves that frequently reach up to 20 feet (6 m) tall.

Loving the water is just a miniscule part of this extreme sport, though. It also requires patience and years of practice. It's not easy to paddle into waves that are 15–20 feet (4.6–6 m) tall each day. To successfully become a big wave surfer, you must dedicate days, weeks, and years to practicing your technique and studying the greats that came before you. Most importantly, you must know how to read the water and understand how to find the right wave. Without that patience and knowledge, you won't catch that huge surf. You may end up severely injured, or worse.

Just ask Laird Hamilton, an American big wave surfer and one of the geniuses behind big wave surfing—and other **crossover sports**. Many members of the surfing community have praised Hamilton for being a groundbreaking pioneer for big wave surfing. Hamilton is credited with influencing the creation in the 1990s of tow-in surfing, which requires a surfer to be towed in by a jet ski before they attempt to catch a huge wave.

Laird Hamilton in Tahiti

Before tow-in surfing, surfers could not ride waves that were 30–50 feet (9–15 m) tall, so Hamilton's idea to use jet skis further pushed the limits of big wave surfing. He also helped popularize **stand-up paddle boarding** and **hydrofoil boarding**. Without his contributions, it is unclear whether big wave surfing would have grown beyond just being a **microcosm** of traditional surfing and become as extreme and popular as it is today. Jet skis still play an integral role in big wave surfing contests, whether they are used to tow a surfer into a wave or to save a surfer who wiped out. Jet skis have saved the lives of hundreds of professional surfers.

Hamilton—and other big surfing names in the 1990s, such as Dave Kalama, Pete Cabrinha, Darrick Doerner, and Rush Randle—were particularly focused on trying to catch a huge open wave called Peahi, named after an area on Maui, Hawaii, and later nicknamed "Jaws" because of how menacing and deadly it was. Paddling into this massive wave is extremely difficult, so these surfers had the idea to use jet skis to tow each other into it.

Hamilton was always determined to challenge himself and push the sport to a higher level, solidifying his role as one of big wave surfing's most important figures. In fact, *Surfer Magazine* has labeled him as "the sport's most complete surfer, displaying almost unnerv-

Jet skis can maneuver around large waves—provided the rider is paying attention.

ing expertise in a multitude of disciplines, and flat-out surfing's biggest, boldest, bravest, and the best big wave surfer in the world today, bar none."

Some surfing purists aren't as positive about Hamilton and his innovations, as they believe tow-in surfing goes against the traditional surfing methods that had been widely practiced for centuries. However, Hamilton has a different perspective on embracing a new type of surfing. In an interview with the online publication *SURFER*, he states that "Surfing and being in the ocean, it doesn't have to conform to one thing. I think surfing really is, ultimately, a philosophy."

Duke Kahanamoku, Waikiki, 1910

Town & Country Surf Designs
Made in Hawaii
Ben Aipa
NORTH SHORE
Boyz
HANALEI
Sailboards
GLOBE
Live Like Sion

# Buying and Riding a Surfboard

Big wave surfing has become more extreme over the last few centuries, and it has garnered a worldwide following. With surfers chasing larger and more dangerous waves, their surfboards have also had to upgrade constantly. Small, weak surfboards just weren't going to do it, especially for surfers who wanted to ride waves that were 20–30 feet (6–9 m) tall.

**OPPOSITE:** A well-used collection of surfboards

If you want to really hone your surfing skills and conquer the largest waves, you should get a firm understanding of the different types of surfboards and the safest ways to get into the water and start surfing.

The surfboard is one of the most important elements to think about before heading to catch some big waves. There are many key factors to consider before buying a new board. Choosing the right one to suit your needs is crucial to your safety. First off, think about where you are going to surf. What kind of water will you be surfing in? Will it be deep or shallow? Are the waves tame, or is the water a bit rougher? These are all valuable questions to ask.

Generally, you can buy either a new or a used surfboard. You may be tempted to buy a shiny new one right away. This can be good if you are in calmer waters, or if you have had some experience with surfing. However, new boards can get dinged up quickly. Used boards are likely to be less expensive than new ones but they may not be as sturdy. If you buy them online, they may not come as advertised. Talk to a local surf shop owner or another experienced surfer if you are interested. They can walk you through what the best and most durable materials are. **Fins** and **leashes** are also integral parts of a surfboard, as these parts can improve your movement

## The Eddie Aikau Invitational

In the 1970s, Hawaii saw the rise of a natural big wave surfer: Eddie Aikau. A native Hawaiian who would come to define the soul of big wave surfing, Aikau showed fearlessness while dropping into waves that other surfers would never dare attempt. Sadly, Aikau was lost at sea after a shipwreck in 1978. Surfing culture remembers him by hosting a big wave competition at Waimea Bay, Oahu, on the condition that the event can only occur if the waves are 20 feet (6 m) or bigger.

through the water and prevent you from losing your surfboard in rougher conditions.

Let's start by discussing **longboards** and shortboards. Longboards are better for new or casual surfers. Longboards are better than shortboards when it comes to handling smaller waves. Plus, they have more space to lie or sit on. If a surfer is still getting used to staying balanced on a board, then longboards are a smart choice.

On the other hand, once the surfer has grasped the basics of "normal" surfing, they may want to consider a shortboard. Shortboards let a surfer build up speed and ride larger waves much more easily than a longboard. Anyone used to catching big, powerful waves will enjoy a sturdy shortboard. But surfers should not use one until they are comfortable with the ocean and with basic surfing mechanics. Otherwise, they will likely fall off their shortboards quite often.

You want a strong board that won't break apart easily. This is where **hardboards** and **soft tops** come into play. Your surfing goals and experience level will determine what board you should get. Soft tops are generally safer to use and easier to ride because of their soft exteriors. Surfers should use a soft top if they are just starting out. A soft top will allow them to get more comfortable with the water and with basic surfing mechanics. Plus, soft tops are more durable than hardboards. They're less likely to be dented or damaged by rocks or sandbars. Soft tops are a great option for children—but also work for more experienced surfers who want to mix things up.

On the other hand, hardboards are somewhat faster and lighter than soft tops. They are better suited for surfers with more experience. However, they also dent more easily, which is not good for surfing in rocky areas or shallow water. Don't surf in a spot that is

## Hang 10! Or How About 66?

As of 2024, the world's longest surfboard was recorded to be 42 feet (13 m) long. In honor of International Surfing Day, a whopping 66 people stood atop the lengthy board at once on June 20, 2015, in Huntington Beach, California. That's a lot of weight for one surfboard to hold! A jet ski had to tow the record-breaking surfboard, and the people onboard were able to balance on it for an impressive 13 seconds. This feat also broke the previous record for the most people riding a surfboard, which was 47 people, according to Guinness World Records.

too shallow and take good care of your surfboard at all times. You should get a sturdy board bag to protect it from scratches and permanent damage.

It is recommended to buy a wetsuit if the water is cold. Summer is usually the warmest time to go surfing, but the water may still be chilly. You don't want to get too cold or irritate your skin on your surfboard. You should also make sure to get a leash for your surfing adventure, to prevent your board from drifting away if you wipe out. Wax is a great way to maintain a stable grip on your board. Beginners who are afraid of falling off or feel unstable on the board should purchase some wax. A local surf shop owner can provide more helpful tips.

Even the best surfers had someone teach them the basics of surfing. If your parents or siblings have experience with the sport, have them watch you and guide you through the fundamentals. Start by just lying on the board and getting used to how it feels. You are most likely not going to ride into a 20-foot (6-meter) wave and hit an **aerial** on your very first try (although it is possible that at least one individual has done it before). Be sure to brush up on your swimming skills if necessary. Learn how to identify currents, rocks, sea creatures, and other surfers while you are in the water. Finally, almost every surfer will tell you never to turn your back on the ocean, especially if waves are coming.

You are likely to fall into the water once you start kneeling on the board, but eventually you will begin to stand up. Standing up on a board is a big milestone for many young surfers, but it is important to practice. Patience is also a must. Practice standing up quickly from a lying or kneeling position, as if preparing to catch a big wave that is on the way. This is called a pop-up.

To do a pop-up, start in a push-up position. Keep your hands positioned under your shoulders. Quickly push yourself up with your arms. At the same time, bring your back foot forward. Push off with your front foot and stand up. Bend your knees slightly for extra stability.

## Dropping In

While learning to surf, many beginners try to catch as many waves as possible so that they can improve. When paddling for a wave, it's important to be on the lookout for other surfers already on it, as joining them—called "dropping in"— is rude and also can be dangerous. A good rule of thumb is that whoever is paddling closest to the wave's breaking point has the right of way.

The pop-up is a very useful tool for improving one's surfing abilities. However, it is important to remember that it takes a long time to truly master the waves and make a clean exit through a barrel (the curl of a wave). Years of hard work, practice, patience, and research on surfing techniques are all essential. Watching the pros is a must to really rise to the next level. The next chapter will discuss the top surfing competitions in the world. It will also describe how surfing was recently added to the **Olympics** and challenges the world's best surfers face when preparing for such large events.

# A Path to the Olympics

Big wave surfing's popularity has been swelling rapidly since the mid-1900s. The creation of faster, more powerful surfboards made many surfers eager to test their limits and constantly challenge each other to catch bigger waves. This led to the rise of many surfing competitions throughout the world, in California, Hawaii, Australia, Europe, and other locations.

Perhaps surfing's biggest achievement in recent times is the addition of the sport to the Olympics lineup in 2020. The Olympics are an international competition that brings together the best athletes from across the globe to compete for gold. Top surfers campaigned to get surfing added to the Olympics for many years, while other popular surfing competitions emerged in the meantime to fill the gap.

Let's revisit Duke Kahanamoku, the Hawaiian surfing superstar from the early 1900s. He was also a world-class swimmer, particularly in freestyle. Kahanamoku was a three-time Olympic freestyle champion and an avid lover of all water sports. Swimming has always been one of the most exciting and adored events in the Olympic lineup. Seeing athletes from all over the world race in the water became a highly anticipated experience for many people.

Kahanamoku wanted to use swimming's popularity and his incredible surfing skills to increase awareness of big wave surfing throughout the world. He joined forces with other top swimmers and surfers to push for surfing to be added to the Olympic sports list. Despite their efforts, surfing was not included in the events list for many decades.

The omission of big wave surfing from the Olympics led to other large competitions arising. One of the most

Duke Kahanamoku at the 1912 Olympics
FOTO MALMSTRÖM
STOCKHOLM 1912

Large crowds gather to watch WSL competitions.

prestigious surfing competitions is the World Championship Tour, which was founded by the World Surf League (WSL) in 1976. This tour is actually a series of different big wave surfing events, held in various locations throughout the year. It brings together the best surfers in the world to compete and test their skills against some truly gigantic waves.

Formerly known as International Professional Surfers (IPS), the WSL was created by Hawaiian surfers Randy Rarick and Fred Hemmings. The two wanted to organize a series of big wave surfing events through an international ranking system. Surfers accumulate points at each of these WSL-sanctioned competitions based on speed, skill, wave size, and other factors, which determine their overall worldwide ranking. The WSL is now considered to be the official world governing body for the sport of surfing.

In the continental U.S., there is also the U.S. Open of Surfing, which was set up in 1959. Today, it is a part of the WSL qualification process. California's Huntington Beach is the site for this massive event, and it is a popular gathering for those who cannot afford to fly overseas to Hawaii, Australia, or other top surf spots. The Quiksilver Pro Gold Coast competition has become another key part of the WSL. Founded in 2002, it's held on Australia's Gold Coast. This area has large, powerful

## The First of Many

The first major surfing competition was held all the way back in 1928. This groundbreaking event was the Pacific Coast Surf Riding Championships, and it lasted until 1941. It was akin to the surfing races that occurred in 12th-century Hawaii. Surfers would take their boards and run out into the water. They would paddle out to a set point, usually marked by a buoy of some sort. Finally, they would put their surfing skills to the test and try to catch the biggest, strongest wave back to the shore. Like older races, the first person whose surfboard would touch the sand would be declared the winner.

Surfers competing hard can suffer some intense wipeouts.

waves that are perfect for some radical surfing.

Another big competition is the Vans Triple Crown of Surfing, founded in 1983. It is actually a combination of three separate events. These esteemed surfing tournaments take place in Oahu, the sport's original home.

Dozens of other competitions take place each year in places such as Portugal, Tahiti, Brazil, the Netherlands, Canada, and more. Across all seven continents, big wave surfing and the thrills of seeing world-class athletes ride massive waves drew in more and more curious spectators. This rise in interest over many years finally led to surfing being included in the official 2020 Olympics events list. (The 2020 Olympics were delayed until 2021 because of the COVID-19 pandemic.)

One fear that held the organizers of the Olympics back from adding surfing was the difficulty of finding locations with large waves. Most Olympic games had been hosted in places with no easy access to the ocean. Traveling to an ocean would have been expensive and time-consuming. However, Japan, the 2020 Olympics host, is a country consisting of many islands. Its capital Tokyo is just a short drive from the beach, where many large waves would make for a successful and exciting surfing competition.

The world's biggest sports gathering had some incredible surfers and inspiring stories. Some of the best surfers across the globe, many of whom had qualified for the Olympics by competing in other major surf competitions, came together to conquer the ocean. One man's story stands out, though, as a reminder of both how dangerous big wave surfing can be and how important it is to never give up on your dreams.

Owen Wright from Culburra, Australia, had been training to become a professional surfer since he was a child. His father made life into a bootcamp of sorts, making him practice extremely hard to perfect his

Owen Wright competing in the 2020 Tokyo Olympics

surfing skills. Many years of hard work and patience made Wright into a very good surfer, but on December 10, 2015, tragedy struck. He was surfing at an event in Pipeline, Oahu, when he was hit hard by several waves. The incident left him with severe brain trauma. He was rushed to a nearby hospital, and it was a miracle he survived. Over the next few years, Wright had to work hard to recover his full brain function while also caring for himself and his family. Despite his struggles, he never gave up on his surfing dream.

Wright was miraculously able to surf again and eventually qualified for the 2020 Olympics. He was not very confident the night before his events, but he reminded himself that surfing was his passion. It was what he was meant to do. "I've already beaten several class acts, and as I've racked up the wins, my confidence has soared," he said in his recent book. "Now, entering this final day, surfing no longer seems like a physical and mental exam, but rather something I was born to do, precisely the right delusion to take into competition."

Wright came in third overall in the Olympic competition, beating out Gabriel Medina for the bronze medal. Not too long after this feat, he decided to take a step back from high-level big wave surfing.

The sport was also included in the lineup for the 2024 Olympics hosted by Paris, France. As part of the events, 20 men and 20 women would compete in Teahupo'o, Tahiti, one of the sport's most famous locations. This milestone shows that despite logistical and financial challenges, big wave surfing has become well-known and beloved. Even the Olympics want to show just how thrilling the sport can be.

## An Olympic Wave

Teahupo'o, the site of the 2024 Olympic surfing competition, is home to one of the heaviest waves on the planet. This is called a "slab" wave, which is created by a very rapid decrease in ocean depth, often as a swell coming from deep water meets a shallow reef. This combination results in a thick "lip" of water to come smashing down, often creating barrels, surfing's most appealing challenge.

# Big Waves on the Big Screen

Just as big wave surfing has made its way to the biggest global competitions, it has also made its way onto the big screen many times in recent decades. Many surfing films tell the stories of the world's most successful big wave surfers. The films usually document surfers' childhoods, love for the water, and how they grew to become great surfers. For many viewers, these stories serve as an inspiration.

**OPPOSITE:** The surf location Mavericks in California was featured in the 2012 film *Chasing Mavericks.*

Take *The Other Side of Fear,* for example. It introduces viewers to big wave surfer Mark Matthews, who nearly lost his life in 2016. He was catching some 6–8-foot (1.8–2.4-meter) waves in New South Wales, Australia, when he was caught in a wave and landed on some rocks, feet first. His legs were severely injured, and one of them nearly had to be amputated. Matthews hopes to surf again one day, despite nerve damage in his legs—but his story is also just one of many reminders that big wave surfing is a very risky sport.

Or how about *Take Every Wave: The Life of Laird Hamilton*? This 2017 documentary film by Rory Kennedy explores the life and career of Laird Hamilton, who, as stated earlier, is largely credited with the creation of tow-in surfing. The film shows Hamilton's ambitious, rebellious nature as a child. It follows him

Hawaiian surfers in 1906, as captured by Thomas Edison

## Oldest Film on Surfing

Thomas Edison, widely known as the inventor of the light bulb, was also a filmmaker. His film studio made more than 1,200 films after it started in the 1890s. Edison produced a black-and-white film in 1906 called *Hawaiian Islands*. Since Hawaii had been annexed to the U.S. in 1898, Edison wanted to show what life was like for native Hawaiians. The three-part film has a lot of footage of Hawaiians surfing at Waikiki Beach, Oahu, showing how important surfing is in Polynesian culture. The film is possibly the oldest surfing footage ever created.

Laird Hamilton (right) with Greg Noll (left). Noll was one of the pioneers of big wave surfing in the 1950s.

through his groundbreaking surfing career and highlights his contributions to the sport. Hamilton may not be loved by everyone, but no one can deny his impact on the surfing community.

T*ake Every Wave: The Life of Laird Hamilton* shows an example of how being a great surfer starts with determination and an undying love for the ocean. Anyone hoping to become a big wave surfer would likely learn from this film. Even children can learn about how to get into that surfer mindset and tackle any challenge.

An image used to promote the iconic 1966 surf movie *The Endless Summer*

Another popular surfing flick is *The Endless Summer*. This 1960s classic film documents two surfers' journey around the world to find "the perfect wave." Michael Hynson and Robert August visit Australia, South Africa, Hawaii, and other locations to find the elusive wave, the huge one that would immortalize them forever. This film

"THE FILM SHOWS THAT IT TAKES A LONG TIME, USUALLY MANY YEARS, TO MASTER ONE'S SURFING TECHNIQUE."

shows that it takes a long time, usually many years, to master one's surfing technique. A surfer must be patient to find the right surfing spot and safely ride tall waves. It is a journey, but with the right people by one's side, anything is possible.

Other movies and documentaries—such as *Riding Giants* (2004), *Surfwise* (2007), *Paradigm Lost* (2017), and *White Rhino* (2018)—give audiences a deeper look into the lives of the world's best big-wave surfers: Laird Hamilton, Jeff Clark, Dave Kalama, Derrick Doerner, Kalani Chapman, and more. And who could forget 2011's *Soul Surfer*, which was based on a true story? Though not solely centered around big wave surfing, this film demonstrates how Bethany Hamilton, an up-and-coming star female surfer, was able to make an impact on the world through means other than surfing. After she lost an arm to a shark attack, she dedicated her life to helping others while also trying to slowly get back into the sport. She traveled to Thailand to aid the victims of a 2004 Indian Ocean tsunami and helped children overcome their fear of the ocean.

Many surfing movies, documentaries, and TV programs show that big wave surfing is not just about

Bethany Hamilton

# The Quest for a 100-Foot Wave

In 2011, renowned big wave surfer Garrett McNamara broke the world record for largest wave ever surfed off the coast of Nazaré, Portugal. The wave was estimated at 78 feet (24 m) high. He has continued searching for even larger waves in the same location, which is well suited for such large swells due to a massive underwater trench, or dip in the ocean floor, located just offshore. After McNamara proved surfing these monster swells was possible, it became the aspiration of many big wave surfers. The Guinness World Record is now held by Sebastian Steudtner, who managed to ride an 86-foot (26-meter) wave, also in Nazaré.

Pedro Calado of Brazil catches a massive wave in Puerto Escondido, Mexico.

seeing people ride waves the size of a skyscraper. It's not only about sitting and waiting and practicing how to catch "the perfect wave." Surfers are real people with interesting, powerful stories. Sharks, rocks, jet skis, and monster waves all pose deadly threats to these men and women, yet they have the strength and willpower to keep heading out into the water.

Big wave surfing is both a mental and physical battle. With great risk, though, come even greater rewards and satisfaction. While there may be a big cash prize or eternal fame in the surfing community, the thrill of a perfect wave—as well as being able to make an impact on a novice aspiring surfer—is what keeps a surfer going. There is always something for professionals to work hard for, and always another wave to be found. Most, if not all of them, will tell you that you can get to a high level in the surfing world, conquer your fears of the ocean, and do just about anything. It's all about having the patience and fortitude to not give up, to keep getting back up on the surfboard even when giant waves keep knocking you down. This was what kept Laird Hamilton going in his prime, and it can keep you going too.

Big wave surfers enjoy spectacular views, in addition to adventures.

# Selected Bibliography


Borra, Julian and Laird Hamilton. *Liferider: Heart, Body, Soul, and Life Beyond the Ocean.* Rodale Books, 2019.

Brander, Rob. *Dr Rip's Essential Beach Book: Everything You Need to Know about Surf, Sand and Rips.* UNSW Press, 2010.

Clark, John R.K. *Hawaiian Surfing: Traditions from the Past.* University of Hawai'i Press, 2011.

Gisado, Raul. *Art of Surfing: A Training Manual for the Developing and Competitive Surfer (Surfing Series).* Falcon Guides, 2011.

Lenny, Kai. *Big Wave Surfer: The Greatest Rides of Our Lives.* Rizzoli, 2021.

Long, John. *The Big Drop: Classic Big Wave Surfing Stories.* Falcon Publishing, 1999.

Warren, Andrew, and Chris Gibson. *Surfing Places, Surfboard Makers: Craft, Creativity, and Cultural Heritage in Hawai'i, California, and Australia.* University of Hawai'i Press, 2014.

Wright, Owen. *Against the Water: A surfing champion's inspirational journey to Olympic glory.* Simon & Schuster Australia, 2023.

# Glossary

**adrenaline** a substance produced by the body, often when physically or emotionally stressed, characterized by increased blood flow and heightened excitement

**aerial** a surfing maneuver during which a surfer successfully hits the crest of a wave and goes up into the air. This is usually a scoring criterion in many surf competitions.

**crest** the highest surface part of a wave; the top part that curls over just before breaking

**crossover sport** a sport that uses similar skills to an athlete's main sport

**fin** surfboard accessory that improves stability and makes it easier for surfers to control their board

**hardboard** surfboard with a hard exterior made from a rough material such as fiberglass-reinforced epoxy and polyester resin

**hydrofoil boarding** a type of surfing in which both a surfer and their hydrofoil board rise above the water's surface for greater speeds and maneuverability

**leash** cord that attaches a surfer's ankle to the tail end of a surfboard, to prevent the board from being swept away by waves

**longboard** surfboard that is typically 8 feet (2.4 m) long or longer and around 2 feet (0.6 m) wide. It is the original type of surfboard, dating back to the origins of surfing in ancient Polynesian culture.

**microcosm** something small regarded as having the same features or qualities as something else that is much larger

**Olympics** a set of international sports events that take place once every four years

**shortboard** surfboard that is usually 6–7 feet (1.8–2.1 m) long and about 21 inches (53 cm) wide. It was created in the 1960s.

**shred** in surfing, to surf a wave in a skillful way

**soft top** surfboard with a softer exterior typically made from a material such as foam

**stand-up paddle boarding** a water sport in which surfers stand on a surfboard and use a paddle to propel themselves through the water

**swell** a self-sustaining wave generated by energy beneath the ocean's surface

**trough** the lowest part of a wave

**tsunami** a large and powerful wave caused by an earthquake, landslide, volcanic eruption, or another underwater disturbance

**wipe out** to fall or be knocked off a surfboard, usually when hit by a wave

# Websites

### History of Big Wave Surfing: From the Roots to Today

https://www.redbull.com/us-en/history-of-big-wave-surfing

Learn more details about the top surfers that made this extreme sport so popular and how it has exploded in popularity since the 1950s.

### World Surf League

https://www.worldsurfleague.com/

The official website of the World Surf League (WSL) includes news, surfer biographies, surfing competition results, photos, videos, merchandise, and more.

# Index